YESTERDAY'S CHARM

TRADITIONAL OR CONTEMPORARY
TECHNIQUES FOR CREATING A MASTERPIECE

Photography—Brian Birlauf
Illustrations and Graphics—Lynn Pike, Sharon Holmes, and Marilyn Robinson
Editing—Sharon Holmes
© 1991 Lynda Milligan and Nancy Smith
Published in the United States of America by *Possibilities*, Denver, Colorado.
ISBN: 0-9622477-8-2
First Printing 1991

YESTERDAY'S CHARM

APPROXIMATE FINISHED SIZE: 67″ x 84″
BLOCK SIZE: 17″
SETTING: Blocks set straight with 8″ quilted border added to each side.
TECHNIQUE: Hand applique, hand embroidery, and hand quilting. Machine applique, fusing web applique, shadow applique, and machine quilting are usable techniques also.

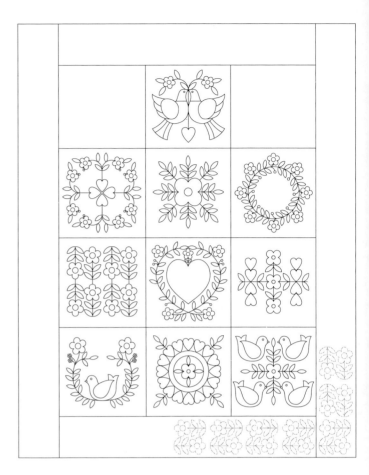

Yardage (42″- 45″ or 107-114 cm wide):

Block background	3¼ yds. (3.0 m)
Small flowers, hearts, & circles	scraps at least 4″ x 4″ to total ¾ yd. (.7 m)
Leaves	scraps at least 1½″ x 2½″ to total ¾ yd. (.7 m)
Large heart	1 scrap at least 10″ x 10″
Large flower	1 scrap at least 6″ x 6″
Small birds/body	5 scraps at least 6″ x 7½″
Small birds/wings	5 scraps at least 3″ x 5½″
Large birds/body	2 scraps at least 5½″ x 7½″
Large birds/wings	2 scraps at least 6″ x 6″
Large birds/head, tail	2 scraps at least 4½″ x 6½″
Circle/ring	1 scrap at least 8½″ x 8½″
Border	2½ yds. (2.3 m)
Binding	¾ yd. (.7 m)
Backing	5⅛ yds. (4.8 m)
Batting	72″ x 90″ (180 cm x 225 cm)

Cutting (¼″ seam allowances included):

Block background	12 blocks 17½″ x 17½″
Border	7 crossgrain cuts 8½″ wide
Binding	8 crossgrain cuts 2½″ wide
Appliques	Refer to *Hand Applique* section of *Quiltmaking Techniques*.

Directions:

Please read all directions before beginning.

1. Fold each 17½″ square in half horizontally, vertically, and diagonally; lightly press in folds. Trace full patterns onto tissue paper reversing images when necessary. Use a light box or tape patterns to a window with good light. Place background fabric over pattern, centering design on pressed lines. Mark pattern as lightly as possible with a #3 pencil. Refer to *Hand Applique* section of *Quiltmaking Techniques* for completing applique.

2. Refer to *Hand Embroidery* section of *Quiltmaking Techniques* for embroidery stitches. Using 3 strands of floss, outline stitch stems and satin stitch berries. Flower centers can be done with satin stitch, with French knots, or as applique. Use outline stitch for tail feathers and satin stitch for eyes and beaks.

3. Assemble blocks referring to *Assembling* section of *Quiltmaking Techniques*. Add borders by referring to *Stairstep Borders* section of *Quiltmaking Techniques*. Piece crossgrain cuts (selvage to selvage) to make the needed lengths. Sew borders to top and bottom first, then sides.

4. Press quilt top well.

5. Mark top for quilting referring to *Marking a Quilt Top* section of *Quiltmaking Techniques*.

6. Refer to *Preparation of Backing and Batting* section of *Quiltmaking Techniques*. Piece backing to 73″ x 90″.

7. Baste quilt referring to *Basting* section of *Quiltmaking Techniques*.

8. Refer to *Hand Quilting* section of *Quiltmaking Techniques*. Quilt around appliques; use the wreath design for quilting the 2 solid blocks at the top of the quilt; fill in the corners of blocks with quilted hearts. Flowers and leaves can also be quilted in the corners of blocks when space allows. The 2 single flowers from block 5 form the border quilting design.

9. Bind quilt referring to *Binding* section of *Quiltmaking Techniques*.

YESTERDAY'S CHARM WALLHANGING

APPROXIMATE FINISHED SIZE: 27″ x 65″
BLOCK SIZE: 17″
SETTING: Three blocks set vertically or horizontally, framed with 2″ sashing, finished with 3″ border. Additional flowers appliqued in border.
TECHNIQUE: Fusible web applique and machine quilting. Hand, machine, or shadow applique can be used also. Stems are drawn with permanent marker but could be hand embroidered.

Yardage (42″- 45″ or 107-114 cm wide):

Block background	1 yd. (1 m)
Flowers & circles	scraps at least 4″ x 4″ to total ½ yd. (.5 m)
Leaves	scraps at least 1½″ x 2½″ to total ⅜ yd. (.4 m)
Hearts	4 scraps at least 3½″ x 3½″
Sashing	⅜ yd. (.4 m)
*Border	⅝ yd. if borders are pieced (.6 m) 2 yds. if not pieced (1.9 m)
Binding	½ yd. (.5 m)
*Backing	2 yds. (1.9 m)
Batting (45″ wide)	2 yds. (1.9 m)
Fusing web	2¼ yds. (2.1 m)

*If border and backing are the same fabric - 2 yds (1.9 m)

Cutting (¼″ seam allowances included):

Block background	3 blocks 17½″ x 17½″
Sashing	5 crossgrain cuts 2½″ wide
Border	5 crossgrain cuts 3½″ wide
Binding	5 crossgram cuts 2½″ wide
Appliques	Refer to *Fusing Web Applique* section of *Quiltmaking Techniques*.

Directions:
Please read all directions before beginning.

1. Fold each 17½″ square in half horizontally, vertically, and diagonally; lightly press in folds. Trace full patterns onto tissue paper. Use a light box or tape patterns to a window with good light. Place background fabric over pattern, centering design on pressed lines. Mark pattern as lightly as possible with a #3 pencil. Refer to *Fusing Web Applique* section of *Quiltmaking Techniques* for completing the applique. Use a light brown, fine permanent marking pen to mark the stems.

2. Sashing: From 5 crossgrain cuts (selvage to selvage), cut 4 pieces 2½″ x 17½″. Set the blocks together with the sashing strips between them and at each end. Measure down the center of your strip of blocks, cut edge to cut edge, to get the length to prepare the side sashing strips. Piece remaining crossgrain cuts of sashing into two strips this length (approximately 59½″) and stitch one to each side of the strip of blocks.

3. Border: Refer to *Stairstep Borders* section of *Quiltmaking Techniques*. Press well.

4. Complete the applique in the border.

5. Mark top for quilting referring to *Marking a Quilt Top* section of *Quiltmaking Techniques*.

6. Refer to *Preparation of Backing and Batting* section of *Quiltmaking Techniques*. Cut backing 31″ x 69″.

7. Baste quilt referring to *Basting* section of *Quiltmaking Techniques*.

8. Refer to *Machine Quilting* section of *Quiltmaking Techniques*. Wallhanging was quilted in the ditch along sashing seams, in straight lines measured in from edges of blocks, in a crosshatch design in the center of the wreath, and ⅛″ outside the larger appliques.

9. Bind quilt referring to *Binding* section of *Quiltmaking Techniques*.

YESTERDAY'S CHARM - Double/Queen

APPROXIMATE FINISHED SIZE: 85" x 105"
BLOCK SIZE: 17"
SETTING: 30 blocks - 14 quilted with wreath pattern, 16 appliqued in pattern of your choice. 3" of background fabric is pieced between top 2 rows for pillow tuck.
TECHNIQUE: Your choice of hand applique, machine applique, fusing web applique, hand or machine quilting.

Yardage (42"- 45" or 107-114 cm wide):
We have figured yardage generously to allow for your personal choice. The minimum amount is listed.

Block background & pillow tuck	8 yds. (2.8 m) 7.4 m
Small flowers, hearts, & circles	scraps at least 4" x 4" to total 1½ yds. (1.4 m)
Leaves	scraps at least 1½" x 2½" to total 1½ yds. (1.4 m)
Large heart - for *each* heart	1 scrap at least 10" x 10"
Large flower - for *each* flower	1 scrap at least 6" x 6"
Small bird/body - for *each* body	1 scrap at least 6" x 7½"
Small bird/wing - for *each* wing	1 scrap at least 3½" x 5½"
Large bird/body - for *each* body	1 scrap at least 5½" x 7½"
Large bird/wing - for *each* wing	1 scrap at least 6" x 6"
Large bird/head, tail - for *each* set	1 scrap at least 4½" x 6½"
Circle/ring - for *each* circle/ring	1 scrap at least 8½" x 8½"
Binding	¾ yd. (.7 m)
Backing (pieced horizontally)	8¼ yds. (7.6 m)
Batting	90" x 108" (225 cm x 270 cm)

Cutting (¼" seam allowances included):
Block background	30 blocks 17½" x 17½"
Pillow tuck	3½" x 85½"
Binding	10 crossgrain cuts 2½" wide
Appliques	Refer to appropriate section of *Quiltmaking Techniques* for the chosen method.

Directions:
Please read all directions before beginning. Choose applique blocks; repeat one design in all the applique blocks in the lower part of the quilt and choose 2 different ones to use across the pillow, or alternate several different blocks in the lower part of the quilt as desired. The wreath design makes a good quilting pattern for the 14 quilted blocks. Refer to directions on page 2 for marking, hand appliqueing the blocks, assembling the quilt, and quilting. If other methods are desired, refer to appropriate sections of *Quiltmaking Techniques*. Follow diagram for placement of pillow tuck. Piece backing horizontally to 91" x 111".

YESTERDAY'S CHARM PILLOWS

Yardage:
Choose from ruffled, corded, or shadow applique styles. Yardage is for one pillow. Buy fabric for ruffle, cording *or* shadow applique.

Block background	½ yd. (.5 m)
Flowers	⅛ yd. (.2 m)
Leaves	⅛ yd. (.2 m)
Hearts	⅛ yd. (.2 m)
Backing	½ yd. (.5 m)
Ruffle	⅞ yd. (.8 m)
Cording fabric	⅓ yd. (.3 m)
Cording #150	2⅛ yds. (2 m)
Organza or other sheer fabric	½ yd. (.5 m)

Directions:
Cut 17½" x 17½" squares of background and backing fabrics. Follow directions for marking in step 1 of directions for quilt on page 2. Follow directions for hand applique, machine applique, fusing web applique or shadow applique in appropriate sections of *Quiltmaking Techniques*. Follow directions for making the pillow in *Ruffled or Corded Pillow* section of *Quiltmaking Techniques*.

FABRIC PREPARATION

Fabrics of 100% cotton are highly recommended for quilting. All washable fabrics should be laundered before being used in a quilt. Determine if fabrics are colorfast by handwashing separately in detergent and warm water. If the water remains clear, fabrics may be washed together. If any fabric bleeds, wash it separately. If fabric continues to bleed, discard and select another fabric. After checking for colorfastness, wash fabrics in a washing machine with warm water and a mild detergent; rinse well. Since most shrinkage occurs in the dryer, tumble until nearly dry. Press using steam and spray sizing if necessary.

HAND APPLIQUE

1. Make templates from patterns without adding seam allowances.
2. Place template down on *right* side of fabric and draw around it.
3. Cut pieces out by cutting ³⁄₁₆″ to ¼″ *outside* of drawn line.
4. Baste under all edges that are not overlapped by another piece by folding edges under on penciled line and basting in place with a single thread.
   a. Clip seam allowance on inside curves allowing fabric to spread.
   b. Clip inside angles up to seamline. When appliqueing these angles, take small overcast stitches to prevent fraying.
   c. Miter outside points less than 90° in three separate folds: Fold down point; fold one edge to seamline; fold other edge to seamline. It may be necessary to trim corner before folding to reduce bulk.

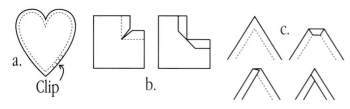

5. Pin or baste pieces to background fabric using pattern as a guide.
6. Applique with matching thread. Work stitches from right to left. Hide knot under applique or on back. To begin, bring needle up through applique and out the edge of the fold. Directly below where thread emerges from applique, take a tiny stitch through the background fabric, bringing needle point immediately back up into the fold of the applique. Run the needle point along inside the fold for ⅛″ to ¼″ and then out through the edge of the fold. Pull thread through. Repeat. Do not press applique pieces.
7. If the work is to be quilted, it is much easier and usually looks nicer if the backing fabric is removed from behind the larger applique pieces. Working from the wrong side with small, sharp scissors, carefully cut away the backing fabric up to ¼″ from the applique seamline. This also helps avoid the possibility of a darker background fabric showing through a lighter applique shape.

HAND EMBROIDERY

1. The stem or outline stitch is used for fine lines. Work left to right, inserting the needle a short distance to the right and bringing it up to the left at a slight angle. For stem stitch, keep thread below needle; for outline stitch, keep thread above needle.
2. The satin stitch is used to cover small background areas. Bring the needle up at one edge; insert at opposite edge. Return to starting edge, carrying needle under fabric. The padded satin stitch is done by working a second layer of satin stitches over the first but in the opposite direction.
3. The French knot is a small decorative knot used for filling space or accenting an area. Bring needle up through fabric; wrap thread around needle. Hold wrapped thread in place while inserting needle into fabric close to where thread emerged. Draw thread down through knot.

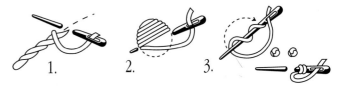

MACHINE APPLIQUE - Fusing Web Method

1. Trace patterns onto smooth, paper side of fusing web. *Trace patterns the reverse of the direction wanted.*
2. Press fusing web to wrong side of desired fabric with rough side facing fabric. Cut out shapes.
3. Peel off paper; position applique onto background fabric and press again; applique fuses to background. If design is layered, arrange all appliques before fusing.
4. Place typing paper or tear-away stabilizer under background fabric. Use a very short stitch length and a ¹⁄₁₆″ to ⅛″ wide zig-zag stitch width. Use a good quality thread. Loosen top tension as needed to keep bobbin thread from being visible on top of work. Keep the threads of the satin stitch at right angles to the edge of the applique by pivoting as needed. To pivot, leave needle in fabric, lift presser foot, turn fabric, lower foot, resume sewing. For outside curves, pivot when needle is on background fabric. For inside curves, pivot when needle is on applique fabric. To make tapered points, reduce stitch width while sewing. To tie off threads, bring stitch width to zero and take six to eight stitches next to the satin stitching. When finished sewing, tear away background stabilizer.

FUSING WEB APPLIQUE

Follow directions above for fusing web method of machine applique, omitting step 4.

SHADOW APPLIQUE

1. Follow steps 1 through 3 of fusing web method of machine applique above.
2. Layer a piece of sheer fabric such as organza over top of fused pieces, trim to same size as block, and baste in place.
3. Lay pieces of backing and batting that are slightly larger than the block down on a flat surface (right side of backing facing down, batting on top). Lay quilt block on top right side up and baste in place.
4. Quilt next to outside edges of fused appliques.

ASSEMBLING THE QUILT TOP

1. Sew all block units together into rows using a ¼″ seam allowance. Press all seams between block units of odd rows (one, three, five, seven, ...) to the right and all seams between block units of even rows (two, four, six, eight, ...) to the left. When rows are sewn together, seams will butt up against each other and hold each other in place for machine sewing.
2. Sew row one to row two, row three to row four, row five to row six, and so on. Sew row unit one-two to row unit three-four and so on. When sewing row *units* together, there will be less bulk than when sewing individual rows together in order. The final row seam will connect the top half of the quilt to the bottom half.

STAIRSTEP BORDERS

1. To determine the length of the top and bottom borders for any assembled quilt center, measure the width of the quilt from cut edge to cut edge at intervals and take an average of these measurements. *Do not* use top or bottom edge as one of the measurements.

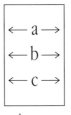

$$\frac{a+b+c}{3} = \text{width}$$

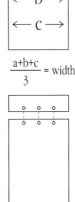

2. Piece crossgrain cuts (selvage to selvage) of fabric to equal the average width of the quilt center or cut seamless borders from fabric on the lengthwise grain. Fold the border and the quilt top into quarters and mark with pins. Matching marker points, pin border to quilt right sides together. If one edge (quilt top or border) is slightly longer, put the longer edge against the feed dog, and the excess fabric will be eased. Take care to see that the pressed seams of the quilt top and border lay flat and do not get twisted.
3. Repeat above process for side borders.
4. Press border seams toward the outside edges of the quilt unless show-through can be prevented by changing pressing directions of border seams.

MARKING A QUILT TOP

1. If possible, mark quilting designs on the right side of the quilt top before layering it with backing and batting. It is much easier to work on a hard, flat surface.
2. Quilting designs can be taped to a window with good light. Hold quilt top in position over design and mark lightly with a pencil. Sometimes it is possible to mark quilting designs before the quilt blocks are assembled, which makes marking easier.
3. Many designs can be marked by making a template of the repeated shape. Be sure to make notches on the template where the shapes overlap.
4. If using a stencil, mark lightly and carefully. Connect broken lines by marking freehand.
5. To mark for outline quilting, lay ¼″ masking tape along one side of seam and then quilt next to the other edge of the tape. When finished quilting, simply pick up the strip of tape and reposition it for another quilting line.

PREPARATION OF BACKING AND BATTING
Backing

1. Many quilt tops are wider than one width of fabric. Keep in mind that up to three widths of fabric may be necessary and that joining seams may run vertically *or* horizontally. Figure backing measurements on paper before cutting. Be sure to allow extra width and length.
2. Tear or cut off selvages.
3. Stitch pieces together using a ¼″ seam allowance. Press seams open to eliminate bulk if hand quilting.

Batting

1. If using prepackaged batting, choose the correct size needed, remembering to allow *at least* 2″ or 3″ extra at each side of the quilt.
2. If using batting sold by the yard, it may be necessary to seam widths together. This is very easily done by butting the batting edges together (not overlapping) and securing them with large, fairly loose whipstitches. Whipstitch on both sides of batting. Take care when quilting not to pull seam apart.

BASTING

1. This step joins the three layers (quilt top, batting, and backing) together in preparation for quilting.
2. Layer the quilt backing (right side down), then the batting, and then the quilt top (right side up). Trim the batting to the same size as the backing.
3. Thread-basting is best for hand quilting projects. Use a long running stitch and catch the three layers every few inches. Start in the center and baste toward the edges in a sunburst design. Roll the backing and batting at the outer edges over to the front; baste in place with large stitches. This will protect the batting. As quilting stitches are added, basting stitches should be removed.

4. Pin-basting can be done with 1″ rustproof safety pins if quilting will be done quickly so they can be removed before they damage the quilt. This method works best for machine quilting. Place pins 4″ to 6″ apart and away from places where quilting lines will be. Edges can be rolled and pinned or left flat.

HAND QUILTING

1. Hand quilting consists of a very tiny running stitch which creates a decorative pattern and holds all three layers of a quilt together. Use a single strand of quilting thread with a tiny knot at one end.
2. Insert the quilting needle through the quilt top and batting but not the backing; bring the needle up where the quilting line will begin. Gently tug the knot so that it slips through the top layer and lodges in the batting.
3. Plant the needle point straight down, lodging the eye end of the needle in one of the thimble indentations, and release the thumb and index finger. To take a stitch, place the thumb on the quilt surface ahead of the  needle point and exert a steady pressure on the needle with the thimble finger to push the needle through the fabric. Rock the needle up and down to take several stitches at one time. Make sure the needle is penetrating all layers by placing a finger of the other hand under the quilt where the needle penetrates the fabric.
4. To end, make a knot that rests on the quilt top close to the last stitch; insert the needle a stitch length away and run it between the layers for a needle's length. Bring the needle back through the top and tug on the thread to pop the knot into the batting. Cut thread.
5. Outline quilting is quilting done ¼″ from seamlines or applique shapes. It avoids seams and shows up well. "Eyeball" the ¼″, use a pencil line, or quilt next to a piece of ¼″ masking tape. Remove tape when not quilting. Quilting "in the ditch" involves stitching very close to the seamline and is nearly invisible from the top of the quilt. Quilt on the side that does not have the seam allowance. It holds the layers together but does not add another design dimension to the quilt.

MACHINE QUILTING

1. Layer backing, batting, and quilt top as in step two in basting section above. Pin-baste with 1″ rustproof safety pins. Place pins other than where quilting lines will be as they are very difficult to remove while quilting.
2. Use an even-feed foot on the machine. Quilting lines should be no more than 4″ apart when using polyester batting.

3. Use poly/cotton or 100% cotton thread on both the top of the sewing machine and in the bobbin or substitute fine transparent nylon thread for the top thread only. When not using nylon thread, it works best to use the same color thread on the top and in the bobbin.
4. Provide support for the quilt to the left and behind the machine in the form of an extra table. Tightly roll the right side of the quilt to fit through the sewing machine. If quilting parallel lines vertically and horizontally, for example, work on the right half of the quilt first, starting at the edge near the center of the top or bottom border; then flip the quilt around 180° and work on the left half. Repeat for horizontal lines.
5. When sewing, hold the work flat with one hand on each side of the machine foot. Try to open the seam slightly when stitching in the ditch (along seamlines) so that when the slight tension is released the stitching "disappears".

BINDING

1. Trim batting and backing even with quilt top.
2. Piece ends of 2½″ wide strips to fit each side of the quilt. Press the binding in half lengthwise wrong sides together.
3. Put binding strips on in the same order the borders were added, usually the side pieces first and then the top and bottom pieces.
4. To apply binding, pin it to the opposite edges of the quilt; pin on the right side and have raw edges even. Stitch using a ⅜″ seam allowance and, if possible, use an even-feed foot to prevent binding from scooting ahead. Bring the binding over the raw edge of the quilt so that the folded edge meets the stitched line on the back. Pin the binding in place on the back of the quilt at each corner.
5. Pin and then stitch the binding to the remaining edges of the quilt as above except allow the binding to extend ½″ at both ends. Turn the extended portion of the binding in before turning it to the back. Handstitch the binding to the back of the quilt at the stitched line.

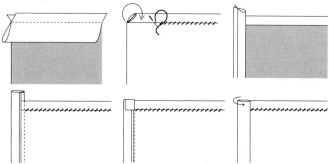

RUFFLED OR CORDED PILLOW

1. Pillow form: Pillow forms may be purchased from fabric and craft stores, or it is very easy to make them. A word of caution about ready-made forms - they are often larger than the size given on the package. If a specific size is needed, be sure to measure the form with a tape measure before

purchasing it. To ensure a smooth pillow, a pillow form about 1″ larger than the desired finished pillow size is needed. To make a form, cut two squares of muslin or needlepunch the size of the pillow top plus 1″. Sew around the four sides of the muslin or needlepunch pieces with a ¼″ seam allowance, leaving an opening on one side. Clip corners, turn, and stuff to desired firmness. Hand or machine stitch opening closed. Insert form into pillow top and add a little extra stuffing to pillow corners if necessary.

2. Cording: Cut a piece of #150 cording equal to the total distance around pillow edge. Cut a bias strip of fabric 1½″ wide by the length of the cording. Lay cording along center of fabric strip on wrong side. Fold fabric over cording, aligning the raw edges. Using a zipper foot, stitch with matching thread using a long stitch length. Sew close to the cord but not too close since it will be sewn to the pillow between this stitching and the cording. Beginning at middle of one side, lay cording on right side of pillow top, all raw edges even. Using a zipper foot and a long stitch length, stitch covered cording to pillow. Stop 1½″ before each corner; make several diagonal cuts into cording seam allowance almost to stitching. Gently curve cording around corners. At the end, cross ends over

each other and finish stitching over cording. Cording can be pulled out and trimmed back to make this crossover lay flat.

3. Ruffle: Measure total distance around pillow edge. At least double that measurement. Cut strips to equal the desired length by double the desired width plus ½″ for seam allowance (i.e., for a 17″ pillow with a 3″ doubled ruffle, cut fabric 68″ x 2 = 136″ long by 2 x 3″ + ½″ = 6½″ wide). Seam shorter pieces together if necessary to make required length. Seam ends of strip together to make one continuous fabric loop. Fold loop in half lengthwise, with right sides out, and press. Run two rows of gathering stitches ¼″ and ⅛″ from raw edges. Fold ruffle into quarters and mark quarter points. With right sides together and raw edges even, pin ruffle to pillow top, matching corners to quarter markings. Pull up gathers evenly, allowing a little extra fullness at corners. Baste in place.

4. With right sides of top and back together, stitch around outer edge of pillow. Leave an opening along one side. Trim corners, turn, and stuff firmly. Whipstitch opening closed.

Block 1
(Continued on page 9)

Center of block

Center of block

Block 1
(Continued from page 8)

Block 2

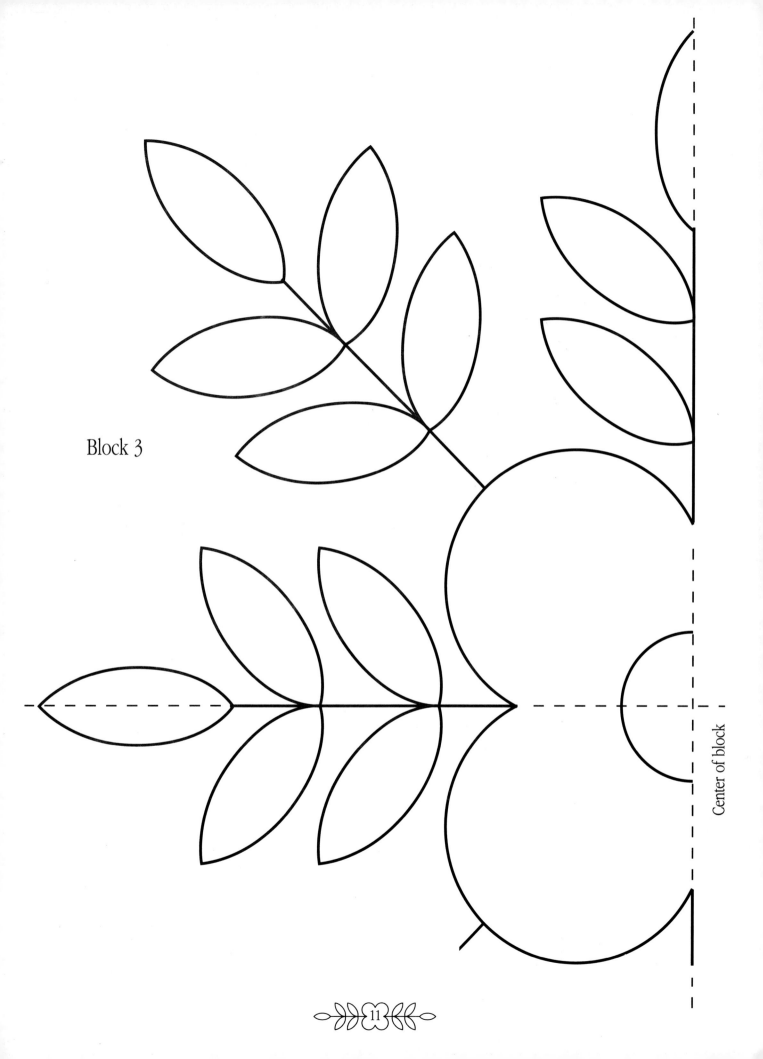

Block 3

Center of block

Block 4

Center of block

Block 5

Center of block

Block 6
(Continued on page 15)

Center of block

Center of block

Block 6
(Continued from page 14)

Block 7

Center of block

Center of block

Block 8
(Continued on page 18)

Block 8
(Continued from page 17)

Center of block

Center of block

Block 8 Bird's Tail

Block 9

Center of block

Block 10

Center of block